STRANGE SCIENCE

HOW DOES IT RAIN FISH?

BY ANNA CLAYBOURNE
AND TIM WESSON

Gareth Stevens
PUBLISHING

Please visit our website, www.garethstevens.com. For a free color catalog of all our high-quality books, call toll free 1-800-542-2595 or fax 1-877-542-2596.

Cataloging-in-Publication Data
Names: Claybourne, Anna. | Wesson, Tim.
Title: How does it rain fish? / by Anna Claybourne and Tim Wesson.
Description: Buffalo, NY : Gareth Stevens Publishing, 2027. | Series: Strange science | Includes glossary and index.
Identifiers: ISBN 9781482478372 (pbk.) | ISBN 9781482478389 (library bound) | ISBN 9781482478396 (ebook)
Subjects: LCSH: Earth sciences--Juvenile literature. | Earth sciences--Miscellanea--Juvenile literature. | Earth (Planet)--Juvenile literature. | Earth (Planet)--Miscellanea--Juvenile literature
Classification: LCC QE29.C53 2027 | DDC 550.2--dc23

Published in 2027 by
Gareth Stevens Publishing
2544 Clinton St.
Buffalo, NY 14224

First published in Great Britain in 2025 by wayland

Commissioning editor: Melanie Palmer
Designer: Lisa Peacock

Printed in China
CPSIA compliance information: Batch #QS27GS: For further information contact Gareth Stevens at 1-800-542-2595.

Find us on

CONTENTS

THE STRANGE SCIENCE OF PLANET EARTH

Moon
North Pole
South Pole
Hi there! It's me, Professor Splat ... and this ginormous ball of rock, floating around in space, is our home, Planet Earth!
Earth is a giant magnet, 4.5 million years old, and mostly covered in water. And it's the only planet where life exists!
That's what you think!

PECULIAR PLANET

SCIENTISTS STUDY ALL KINDS OF THINGS ABOUT OUR WEIRD AND WONDERFUL WORLD, AND THEY'RE ALWAYS FINDING OUT ALL KINDS OF WACKY STUFF. FOR EXAMPLE, DID YOU KNOW THAT...

• You can do your laundry in a geyser!

Ouch!
Ouch!

• It can rain fish! (And sometimes other animals too.)

• And there are stones that can move around on their own!

How? You're about to find out!

You'll find the answers in these pages! Off we go!

SO MANY QUESTIONS!

WHAT WOULD HAPPEN IF THE MOON DISAPPEARED?

HOW CAN A SHIP SAIL THROUGH THE SKY?

WHAT'S THAT SCARY BALL OF FIRE DOING FLOATING THROUGH MY FRONT ROOM?

I'M THE TALLEST!

IN THE HIMALAYAS, CENTRAL ASIA ...
Welcome to Planet Earth! Of course, you'll want to see all the sights – like the world's highest mountain!
... 29,031 FEET (8,848 M) ABOVE SEA LEVEL
And that would be ME – Mount Everest!
BUT ...
Hmmmmm ... I don't think so!
WHAT! Who's that?
I'm Chimborazo, and I'm actually taller than you. You see ...

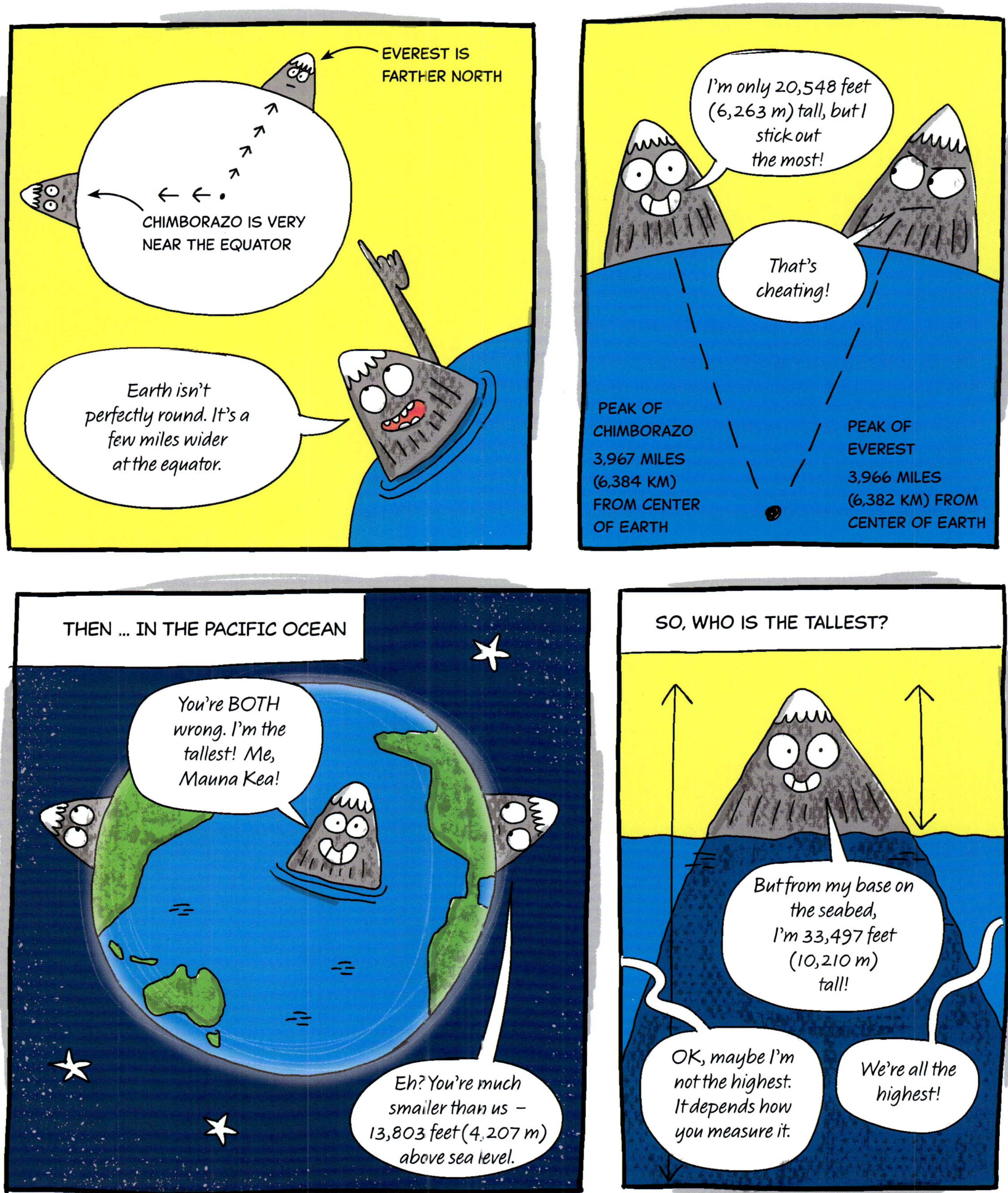
EVEREST IS FARTHER NORTH
CHIMBORAZO IS VERY NEAR THE EQUATOR
Earth isn't perfectly round. It's a few miles wider at the equator.
I'm only 20,548 feet (6,263 m) tall, but I stick out the most!
That's cheating!
PEAK OF CHIMBORAZO
3,967 MILES (6,384 KM) FROM CENTER OF EARTH
PEAK OF EVEREST
3,966 MILES (6,382 KM) FROM CENTER OF EARTH
THEN ... IN THE PACIFIC OCEAN
You're BOTH wrong. I'm the tallest! Me, Mauna Kea!
Eh? You're much smaller than us – 13,803 feet (4,207 m) above sea level.
SO, WHO IS THE TALLEST?
But from my base on the seabed, I'm 33,497 feet (10,210 m) tall!
OK, maybe I'm not the highest. It depends how you measure it.
We're all the highest!

MOVING MOUNTAINS

AS YOU CAN SEE, MEASURING MOUNTAINS ISN'T ALWAYS EASY!

AND THE SAME GOES FOR OTHER PARTS OF EARTH.

FOR EXAMPLE, WHAT'S THE WORLD'S BIGGEST RIVER?

It depends how you measure them!

AMAZON

THE AMAZON, IN SOUTH AMERICA, IS THE WIDEST AND CARRIES THE MOST WATER.

Well, they're BOTH the biggest!

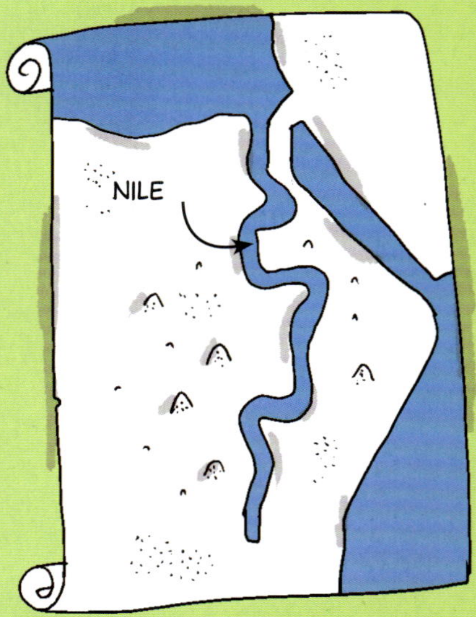
NILE

THE NILE, IN AFRICA, IS THE LONGEST!

CHANGING SHAPE

YOU MIGHT THINK YOU KNOW A FACT... BUT EARTH CAN FOOL YOU!

FOR EXAMPLE, MOUNTAINS CAN CHANGE HEIGHT.

Let's look at Mount St. Helens, a famous U.S. volcano.

9,678 feet (2,950 m) high
MOUNT ST. HELENS BEFORE 1980
BOOM!
MASSIVE ERUPTION IN 1980
8,363 feet (2,549 m) high
MOUNT ST. HELENS AFTER 1980

You're a mountain, not a volcano!
OH NO! I hope that doesn't happen to me!

THE MOON TAKES A TRIP

ONE DAY ...
Goodbye, Earth, I'm off on vacation.
What!? Where?
Oh, just a quick tour of the solar system!
Back soon! Byeee!
Wait! No! You can't do that! I need you!
SO ...
ON THE BEACH
Where's the sea gone? It should be coming back in by now!
BEFORE LONG ...
Help! Without the tide, we're stuck here!
We'll run out of food!
What's happening?

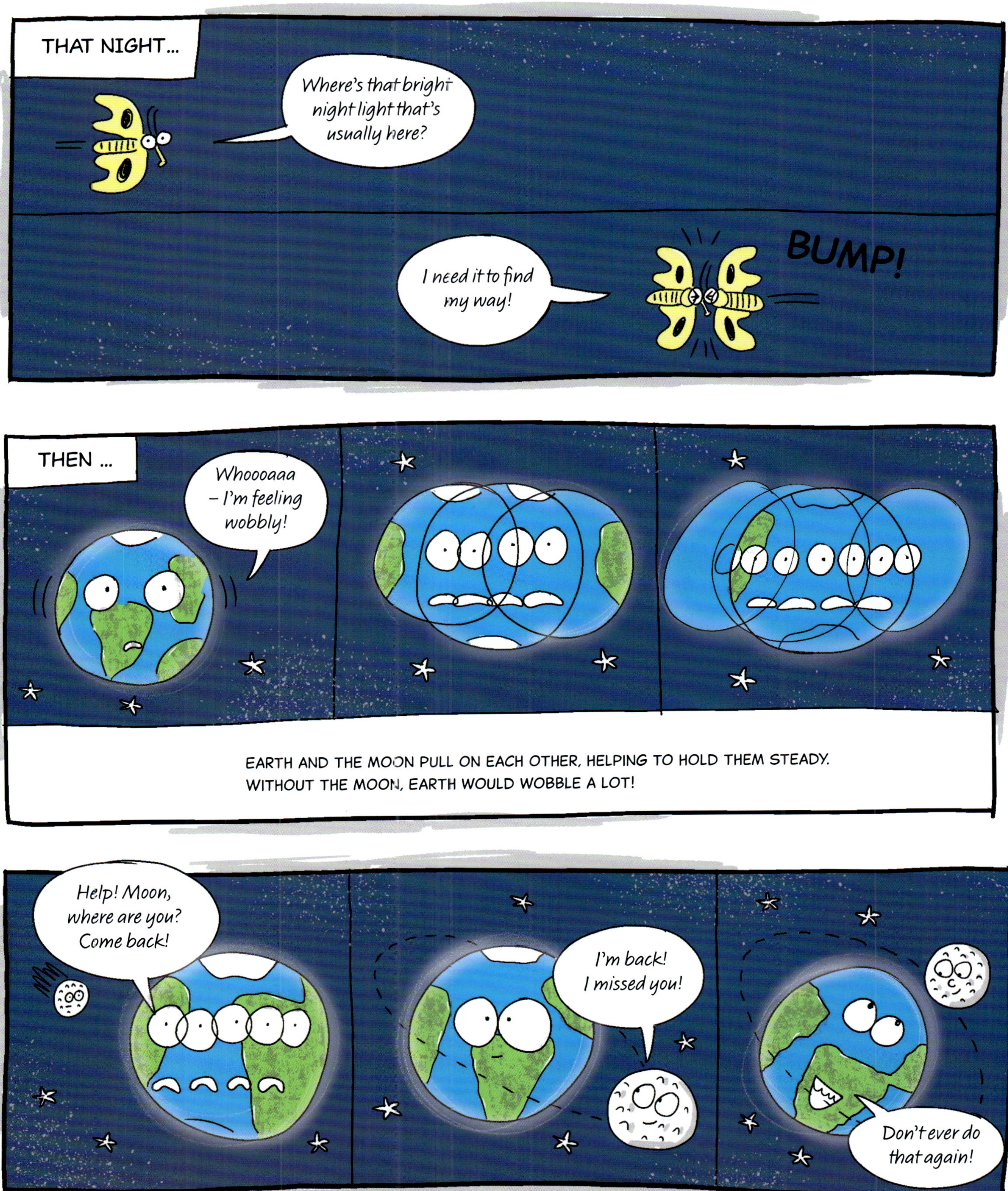
THAT NIGHT...
Where's that bright night light that's usually here?
I need it to find my way!
BUMP!
THEN ...
Whoooaaa – I'm feeling wobbly!
EARTH AND THE MOON PULL ON EACH OTHER, HELPING TO HOLD THEM STEADY. WITHOUT THE MOON, EARTH WOULD WOBBLE A LOT!
Help! Moon, where are you? Come back!
I'm back! I missed you!
Don't ever do that again!

LET'S STICK TOGETHER!

LUCKILY FOR US, THE MOON CAN'T ACTUALLY WANDER OFF INTO SPACE.

If it did, it would be a DISASTER!

THE MOON AND EARTH PULL ON EACH OTHER WITH THE FORCE OF GRAVITY. THIS KEEPS THEM BOTH FROM WOBBLING TOO MUCH.

Moon, we make a great team!

THE MOON'S GRAVITY PULLS THE SEA, GIVING US HIGH AND LOW TIDES AS EARTH SPINS AROUND.

Before streetlights, people relied on moonlight to see their way at night.

AND THE MOON GIVES US LIGHT AT NIGHT.

ANIMALS AND THE MOON

OTHER LIVING THINGS NEED THE MOON TOO ...

We use the full moon to time our migrations, so that we all meet up at once to find a mate.

I use moonlight to roll my ball of dung in a straight line, to get home as fast as possible.

HOWEVER ...

THE MOON IS ACTUALLY MOVING AWAY FROM EARTH! BUT VERY, VERY SLOOOOWLY.

I think I'll stick around for now.
The Moon could finally leave Earth behind ... in about 15 billion years!
It gets about 1.6 inches (4 cm) farther away each year.

ROLLING STONES

IN THE DESERT, CALIFORNIA ...
How VERY strange. Every time I visit, the stones have moved!
Look – each stone has left a trail in the mud!
Maybe they're sliding downhill?
Nope – it's totally flat here.
THAT NIGHT...
It's all clear - no one here!
Off we go! Woohoo!
SO ...
Right. I'm going to solve this mystery once and for all.
OK, stones! You're being filmed!
Bah!

LATER ...
PLAYBACK
They ARE moving! How are they doing it?
Hmmm – it's cold and icy. Is that something to do with it?
They've guessed our secret!
You see, we "sailing stones" don't actually move on our own.
When it rains, a thin layer of water collects on the ground ... and freezes at night.
That makes a huge ice sheet, with us stones stuck in it.
The wind makes the ice move around – and it takes us along too!
Wheeeeee!

ROCK 'N' ROLL!

IT'S NOT NORMAL FOR STONES TO WANDER AROUND ON A FLAT DESERT, CARRIED BY ICE. IT'S VERY RARE.

The "sailing stones" baffled scientists for years!

ROAMING ROCKS

BUT IT **IS** NORMAL FOR ROCKS TO MOVE. THEY'RE DOING IT ALL THE TIME! WIND, RAIN, AND ICE MAKE ROCKS ON CLIFFS AND MOUNTAINS CRUMBLE AND WEAR AWAY.

Heeeeelp!!
DANGER
FALLING ROCKS

RIVERS AND OCEAN WAVES ROLL AND BASH ROCKS AROUND, SMOOTHING THEM INTO PEBBLES.

YOU'RE STANDING ON A PLATE!

THE GROUND WE STAND ON MIGHT SEEM FIXED AND SOLID – BUT IT'S MOVING TOO!

EARTH HAS CRUST, OR OUTER LAYER OF SOLID ROCK.
IT'S MADE OF GIANT SECTIONS, CALLED PLATES.
AND THEY ALL SLOWLY MOVE AROUND.

SCRUNNCH!
RUMBLE!

They move about as fast as your fingernails grow. Sometimes they scrape or crunch together, causing an earthquake.

Arrgh! Run!

IT'S RAINING FISH!

Yum, double helping of breakfast for me!
I'm bored, I want to go somewhere new.
I sense a storm! Come up, and I'll take you somewhere safe!
I'm not falling for that trick – I'm not your dinner! I'm staying here where it's safe.
You're making me dizzy!
Urgh, I ate too much breakfast!
What's happening!
It must be aliens sucking us up to their ship!

Wow! Who knew there was so much land!
And air!
I feel like a fish out of water.
Why are we falling?
This is going to get bumpy!
I will never complain about being bored again!
FINALLY ...
No more air miles for me.
I feel much safer here!

WEIRD WEATHER

NORMAL RAIN IS STRANGE ENOUGH. SQUILLIONS OF DROPS OF WATER, SUDDENLY FALLING OUT OF THE SKY, AND LANDING ON YOU ... IT WOULD SEEM VERY STRANGE IF YOU WEREN'T USED TO IT!

But even stranger, it can actually rain FISH instead of water!

And it's not just fish! It has also rained ...
Jellyfish!
Frogs!
Toads!

YES, REALLY!

YES, IT REALLY CAN RAIN FISH! THERE HAVE BEEN MANY EXAMPLES OF THIS THROUGHOUT HISTORY – EVEN IN ANCIENT TIMES.

ANCIENT GREEK WRITER ATHENAEUS
In ancient Greece, it once rained fish for three days!

Yikes!

BUT HOW?

THE WEIRD RAIN PROBABLY HAPPENS AFTER A TORNADO – A POWERFUL WHIRLING WINDSTORM – MOVES OVER WATER.

Then they fall out of the sky like rain!

THE STRONG WIND SUCKS WATER UP INTO THE SKY – ALONG WITH ANY ANIMALS THAT ARE IN IT!

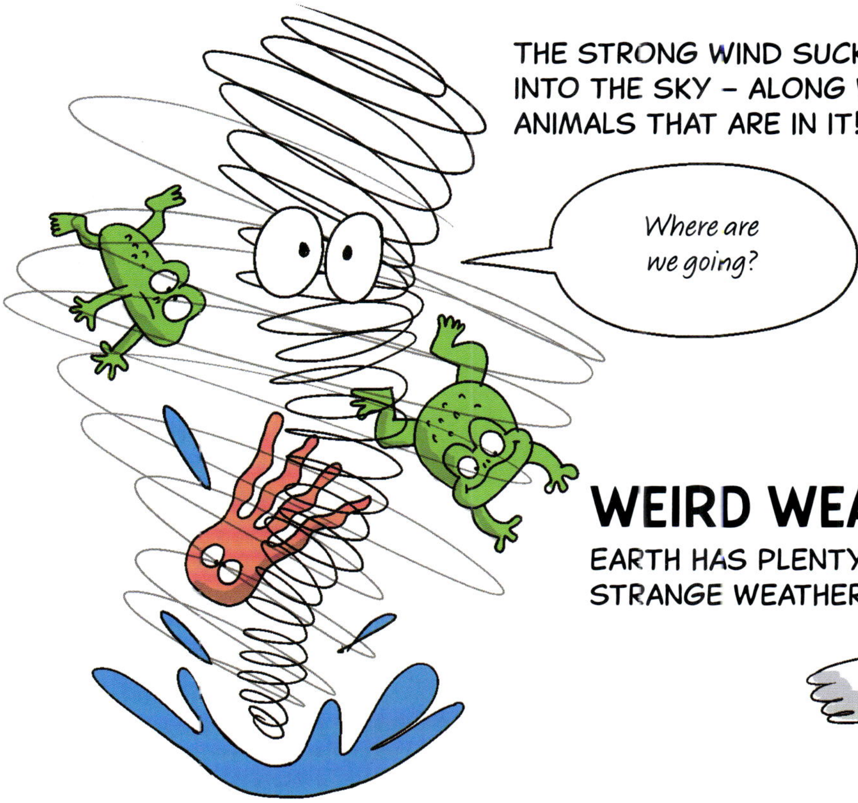
Where are we going?

WEIRD WEATHER

EARTH HAS PLENTY OF OTHER STRANGE WEATHER TOO. LIKE ...

LENTICULAR CLOUDS, WHICH LOOK LIKE FLYING SAUCERS.

MOONBOW – A RAINBOW AT NIGHT, MADE OF MOONLIGHT.

AND BALL LIGHTNING!

What's that? Turn the page to find out!

SMALL BALLS OF FIRE!

PARIS, FRANCE, 1852. A TAILOR IN HIS APARTMENT.
CRASH!
BOOM!
Good thing I work from home.
THEN ...
WHAT is THAT??!!!
SIZZLE!
THEN ...
It's FLOATING! What can it be?
THE THING LOOKED LIKE A GLOWING BALL OF FIRE, THE SIZE OF A HUMAN HEAD!

NEXT...
Arrgh, it's coming to get me!
Don't touch me!
THE BALL ROSE UP INTO THE AIR ...
Now what's it doing??!
FIZZLE!
... BEFORE DISAPPEARING BACK INTO THE FIREPLACE.
Yikes!
Phew! I think it's gone!
WHOOSH!
CRASH!
BANG!!
Help! I think the chimney just exploded!

FRIGHTENING LIGHTNING

WHAT WAS THE STRANGE SIGHT THE TAILOR SAW? IMAGINE THAT HAPPENING TO YOU!

It might seem impossible ... even magical! But it's not. The floating, sizzling, glowing globe was ball lightning!

LIGHTNING IN A BALL?

NORMAL LIGHTING IS SCARY ENOUGH. IT'S A GIANT ELECTRIC SPARK THAT HAPPENS WHEN STATIC ELECTRICITY BUILDS UP IN THUNDERCLOUDS.

ZZZAP!

IT CAN STRIKE TREES, HOUSES, OR SOMETIMES EVEN PEOPLE.

Yes, it's pretty dangerous!

BUT AT LEAST IT DOESN'T USUALLY COME DOWN YOUR CHIMNEY!

BALL LIGHTNING CAN DO THAT.

WHAT IS IT?

BALL LIGHTNING IS A RARE, SLOW-MOVING, FLOATING, GLOWING BALL, SOMETIMES SPOTTED DURING THUNDERSTORMS. THE TAILOR'S LUNCHTIME FRIGHT WAS JUST ONE OF MANY EYEWITNESS ACCOUNTS ...

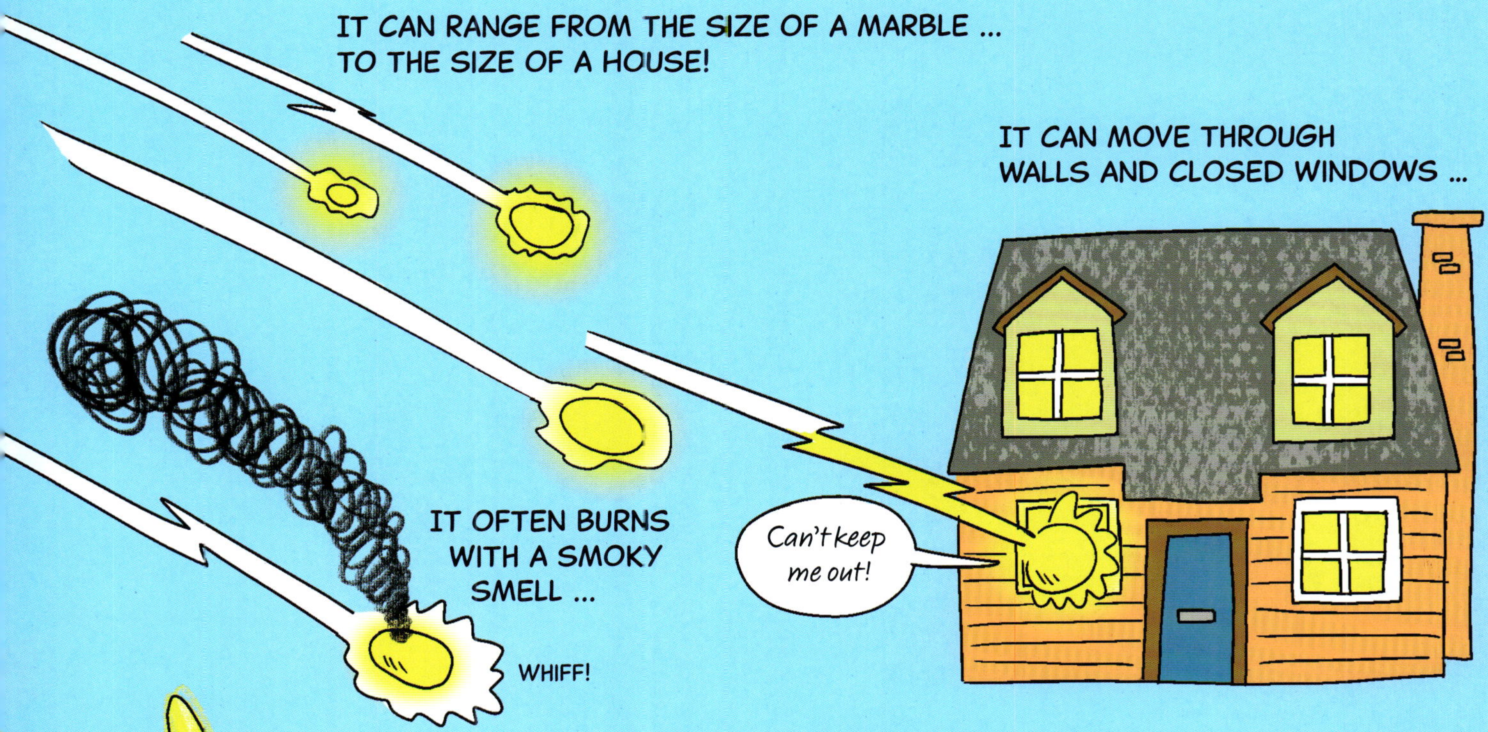
IT CAN RANGE FROM THE SIZE OF A MARBLE ...
TO THE SIZE OF A HOUSE!
IT CAN MOVE THROUGH WALLS AND CLOSED WINDOWS ...
IT OFTEN BURNS WITH A SMOKY SMELL ...
WHIFF!
Can't keep me out!

Pop!
BANG!

... AND IT SOMETIMES EXPLODES!

IT'S A MYSTERY...

HOWEVER, SCIENTISTS STILL DON'T REALLY KNOW HOW BALL LIGHTNING WORKS OR WHAT MAKES IT HAPPEN.

Don't worry, we're working on it!

GUESS THE GEYSER

SOMEWHERE IN THE WORLD, NEAR A VOLCANO...
Here we go ... I think I'm about to erupt!
RUMBLE!
BUBBLE!
IT'S A GEYSER – A NATURAL HOT SPRING ...
THEN ...
WHOOSH!
SPLOSH!
... THAT REGULARLY EXPLODES, SHOOTING HOT WATER INTO THE AIR!
BEFORE LONG ...
Wow, look at that! SPLASH!
It's boiling hot!
Hey, let's wash our clothes in it!
SO ...
There we are!
Now let's see what happens ...
5 MINUTES LATER ...
Oh no! I loved that jacket!
That didn't work!
Our clothes are gone forever!

THEN ...
Maybe it just needs a bit of soap.
SOAP
BOOOMMM!
SUDDENLY...
It worked!
They're clean!
Just need to hang them up to dry!
SPLOOSH!
THEN ...
Maybe this one will clean our clothes too?
Oh no, this is a mud one!

KEEP GEYSERS TIDY!

YES, AS SILLY AS IT MAY SOUND, PEOPLE REALLY DID THROW THEIR LAUNDRY INTO GEYSERS.

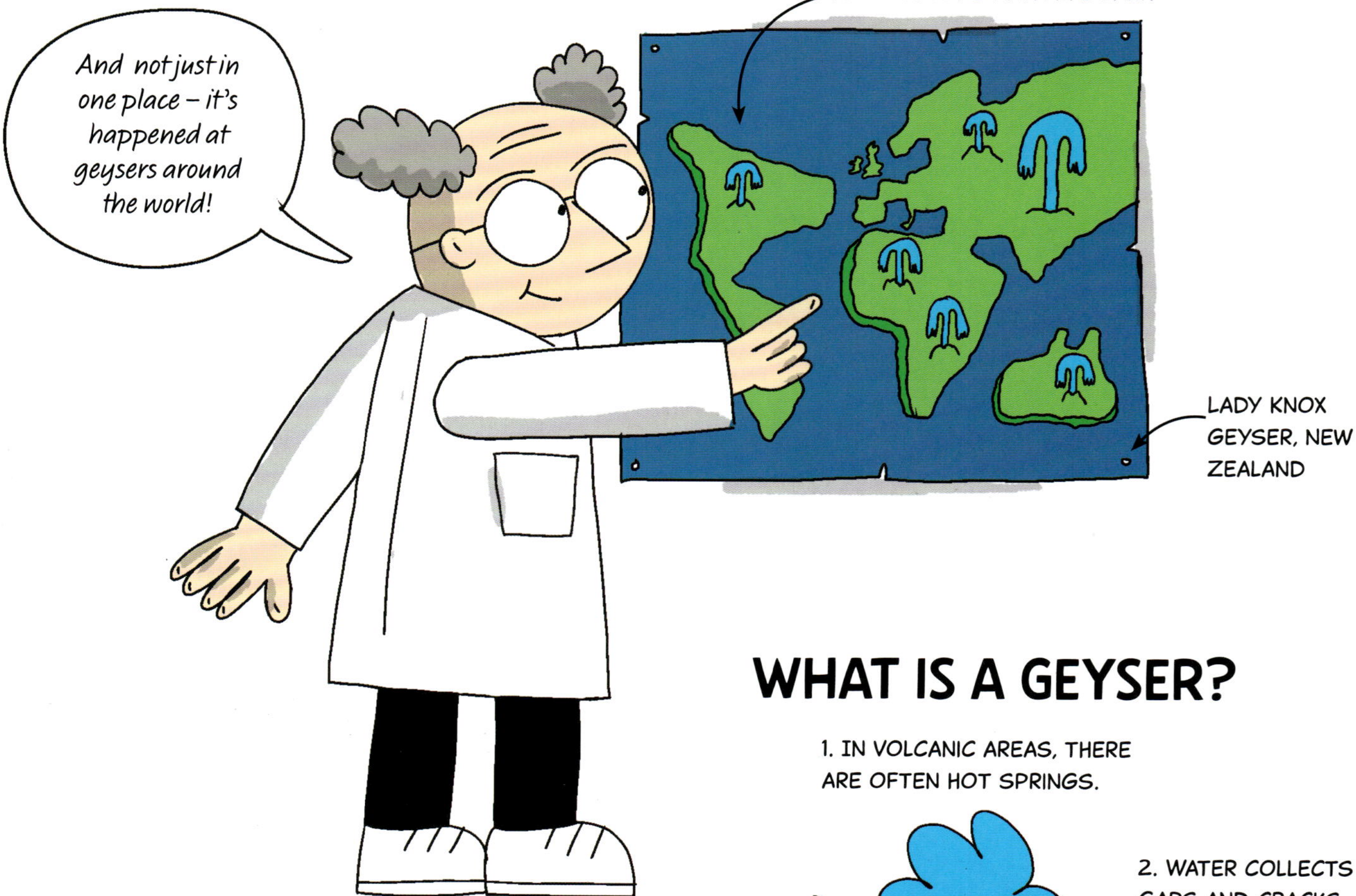
And not just in one place – it's happened at geysers around the world!
OLD FAITHFUL GEYSER, YELLOWSTONE NATIONAL PARK
LADY KNOX GEYSER, NEW ZEALAND

... and probably others too!

WHAT IS A GEYSER?

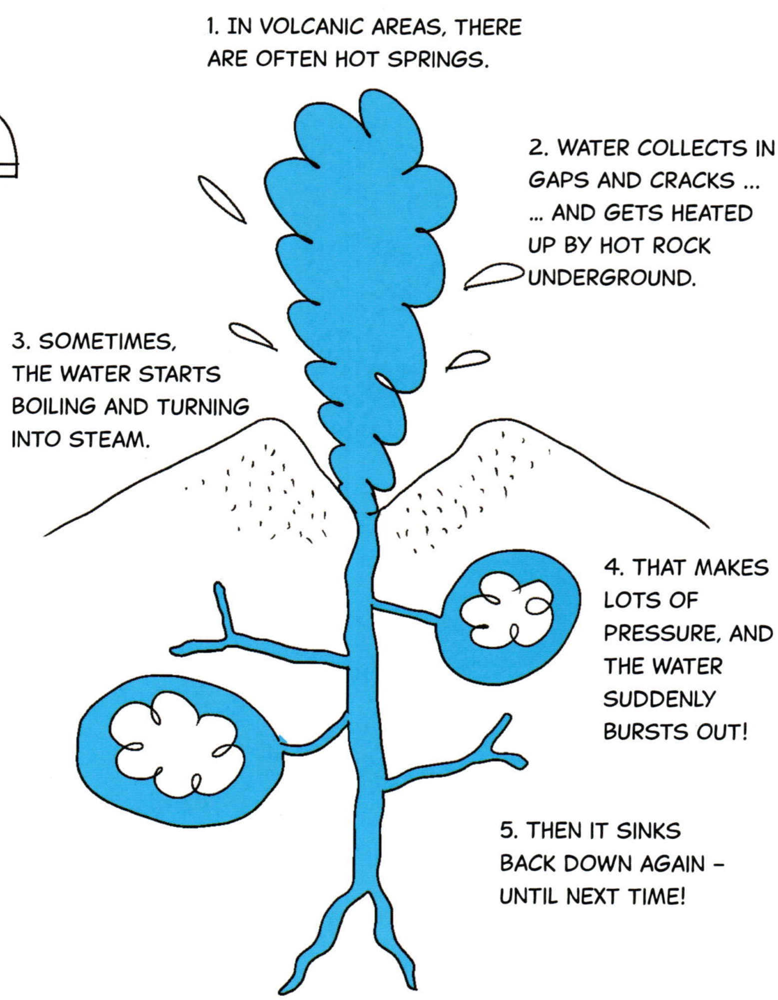
1. IN VOLCANIC AREAS, THERE ARE OFTEN HOT SPRINGS.
2. WATER COLLECTS IN GAPS AND CRACKS ... ... AND GETS HEATED UP BY HOT ROCK UNDERGROUND.
3. SOMETIMES, THE WATER STARTS BOILING AND TURNING INTO STEAM.
4. THAT MAKES LOTS OF PRESSURE, AND THE WATER SUDDENLY BURSTS OUT!
5. THEN IT SINKS BACK DOWN AGAIN – UNTIL NEXT TIME!

SOAP-SPLOSION!

PEOPLE FOUND THAT WHEN THEY THREW SOAP INTO A GEYSER, IT CAUSED AN INSTANT ERUPTION! SOAP IS STILL SOMETIMES USED TO MAKE A GEYSER ERUPT FOR TOURISTS.

The soap makes it easier for the hot steam to push upward.
Watch this!
SOAP
SOAP
WHOOSH!

A STACK IS BORN

ONE DAY ...
Wow! That's amazing!
Take a photo!
That's me! An amazing sea arch! People come from miles around to visit me!
I formed thousands of years ago, as waves washed away the rocks, making this gap.
The gap got bigger and now I'm a beautiful arch!
I keep on changing!
THEN ...
Oh no, it's starting to rain.
It's a storm!

SOON ...
I don't like this! My rocks feel wobbly!
WOBBLE
JIGGLE
SUDDENLY...
Wow! Did you see that! I'm soaked!
Aaaarrggh! What happened!?
NEXT DAY...
I'm not an arch any more! Who's going to visit me now?
BUT...
ANCIENT SEA ARCH FALLS DOWN. NOW WORLD'S HIGHEST SEA STACK!
Yay, I'm a stunning sea stack! And I've got more visitors than ever!

SHAPED BY THE SEA

AN AMAZING SEA ARCH BECAME A STUNNING SEA STACK!

It just goes to show that change isn't always bad!
In fact, Earth's land is always changing shape - ESPECIALLY at the coast.

SEASIDE SHAPES

LOOK AT ANY COASTLINE AND YOU'LL SEE SHAPES LIKE THESE – WHICH SCIENTISTS CALL "LANDFORMS."

HEADLAND
ARCH
STACK
STUMP
HEADLANDS ARE MADE OF HARD ROCK THAT WEARS AWAY SLOWLY.
They're all shaped by the waves, wind, and weather.
BEACH
SAND OR PEBBLES GET WASHED UP, MAKING A BEACH

FROM HEADLAND TO STACK ... TO STUMP!

GRADUALLY, HEADLANDS GET NARROWER AS THE WAVES WEAR THEM AWAY.

1. CRASHING WAVES HOLLOW OUT A CAVE.

2. WAVES BREAK THROUGH, FORMING AN ARCH. THE ARCH GETS BIGGER AND THINNER, UNTIL ...

3. ... THE ARCH IS ERODED SO MUCH IT BREAKS AWAY FROM THE HEADLAND. A STACK IS BORN!

4. THE STACK GETS BASHED BY THE WAVES AND EVENTUALLY BECOMES A STUMP!

AMAZING ARCHES AND STUNNING STACKS

Check out these arches and stacks around the world. Maybe you can visit one!

SAIL ROCK, RUSSIA

DUN BRISTE, IRELAND

OLD MAN OF HOY, SCOTLAND

EL ARCO SEA ARCH, MEXICO

STICKY ROCKS

ONE DAY, IN ANCIENT CHINA ...
Nearly finished harvesting for the day!
JUST THEN ...
CLONK!
That's weird! Look – this rock is stuck to my sickle!
Let's see if it sticks to mine ...
It does!
LATER ...
It sticks to my kettle ...
... and my brooch ...
... and my needles.
It always sticks to iron things ...
how strange!

EVENTUALLY ...
I've discovered something amazing!
If you hang the magnetic rock up and let it move freely, it always lines up north to south!
Hmm, there must be a use for this ...
AND THERE WAS!
SO...
The spoon is carved from magnetic rock. It's balanced so it can turn around. The handle always points south and the other end north.
It's brilliant for finding your way or arranging buildings. I call it the South-Pointing Spoon!
LATER STILL ...
This works even better! The wooden fish floats in a bowl of water. Inside the fish is a magnetized needle. I call it the South-Pointing Fish!

EARTH IS A MAGNET!

THE SOUTH-POINTING SPOON AND THE SOUTH-POINTING FISH WERE EARLY VERSIONS OF THE COMPASS.

THE POINTER IN THE MIDDLE IS A MAGNET THAT'S FREE TO MOVE IN ANY DIRECTION
And we still use compasses today!
N
E
W
S
IT ALWAYS LINES UP NORTH TO SOUTH – JUST LIKE THE SPOON AND THE FISH!
OK, this way!

BUT WHY?

WHY DO MAGNETS POINT NORTH AND SOUTH?

MAGNETIC NORTH POLE
MAGNETIC FIELD (WHERE THE MAGNETIC FORCE CAN PULL ON THINGS)
MAGNETIC SOUTH POLE
It's because Earth is a magnet too. A very BIG magnet!

A MAGNET HAS TWO ENDS, OR POLES: NORTH AND SOUTH. EARTH'S MAGNETIC POLES ARE CLOSE TO THE NORTH AND SOUTH POLES.

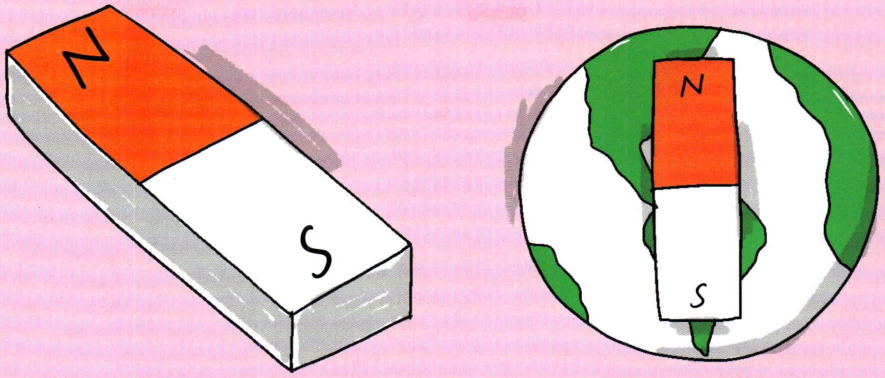

THEY PULL ON THE MAGNET IN A COMPASS, SO IT LINES UP WITH THEM.

MAGNETIC LIGHT SHOW

THE AURORA IS A BEAUTIFUL NATURAL PATTERN OF GLOWING LIGHTS IN THE SKY. IT SOMETIMES APPEARS AROUND THE NORTH OR SOUTH POLE.

IT HAPPENS WHEN A STORM ON THE SUN RELEASES LOTS OF TINY PARTICLES.

EARTH'S MAGNETISM PULLS THEM TOWARD THE POLES, WHERE THEY MAKE THE SKY GLOW.

OVER THE EDGE

NIAGARA FALLS, NORTH AMERICA, 1901 ...
I'll be the first person to ride over Niagara Falls inside a barrel!
Hmm. Is that really a good idea?
BUT...
Yes! I'll be fine.
I'll make my own barrel.
WATERPROOF BARREL
COMFY CUSHIONS
STRAPS FOR STAYING STILL
NEXT...
I, Annie Edson Taylor, will ride over Niagara Falls in a barrel – and survive!
You'll never make it!
It's too dangerous!
As a test, my cat can try it out first!
WHATTT??? Meow!

Meow! Help!
Where am I?
See? The cat's OK!
I'm going ahead!
TWO DAYS LATER ...
OK, see you later!
Good luck!
THE BARREL FLIES DOWN THE FALLS AND INTO THE CHURNING RIVER BELOW!
Aaaarrrrgghh!
How are you feeling, Mrs. Taylor?
AWFUL! That was a REALLY bad idea. No one should ever try that again!
Told you!

GOING WITH GRAVITY

ANNIE EDSON TAYLOR WAS VERY LUCKY TO SURVIVE HER WILD WATERFALL RIDE.

BUT WHY WAS IT SO DANGEROUS?

The clue's in the name! Waterfalls FALL down ...

1. AS THE WATER FLOWS OVER THE EDGE, IT STARTS FALLING, THANKS TO EARTH'S GRAVITY.
2. ALMOST 792,500 GALLONS (3 MILLION L) OF WATER FLOWS OVER THE FALLS EVERY SECOND!
ROAR!
SPLOSH!
NIAGARA FALLS 167 FEET (51 M) HIGH
3. GRAVITY KEEPS PULLING ON IT, MAKING IT FALL FASTER AND FASTER ...
4. IT LANDS WITH SO MUCH FORCE, IT HOLLOWS OUT A DEEP, CHURNING "PLUNGE POOL"

Barrels can easily get trapped underwater in those plunge pools!
I'll stick to land, thanks!

THAT'S WHY RAINWATER FLOWS DOWNHILL, FORMING STREAMS ....

...WHICH JOIN TOGETHER INTO BIGGER RIVERS.

WHERE A RIVER FLOWS OVER A STEEP DROP, YOU GET A WATERFALL!

Like water, rocks, and anything you drop! Oops!

SPLOSH!

EVENTUALLY, WATER FLOWS ALL THE WAY DOWN INTO THE SEAS AND OCEANS.

THEY ARE THERE BECAUSE GRAVITY PULLS WATER DOWN INTO THE LOWEST PARTS OF EARTH'S CRUST.

DON'T TRY THIS AT NIAGARA FALLS!

MANY PEOPLE HAVE DONE DANGEROUS STUNTS AT NIAGARA FALLS – EVEN THOUGH IT'S NOW BANNED. PEOPLE HAVE SURVIVED TIGHTROPE WALKING ACROSS THE FALLS!

Steady ...

WATER ... WATER
SOMEWHERE IN A SCORCHING HOT, DRY DESERT ...
Water ... I need water!
THEN ...
Water! An oasis! Can it be true!?
Wow.
SO ...
Water! Nearly there ...
Not if I get there first!
BUT...
Huh? It's disappeared!
Where is it?

THEN ...
What happened? I saw it with my own eyes – and it vanished! I'll die of thirst!
It was a mirage, of course!
Give me water!
The air close to the ground is very hot. And the air above is cooler. The layers of air bend blue light coming from the sky, so it looks as if there's a blue pool on the ground! But there isn't.
SO...
But I need water!
Oh, why didn't you say!?
Thank you!
Water ...
water ...
There's a real oasis just over there!
SOON ...
Finally! SLURP!

THE MAGIC OF MIRAGES

MIRAGES REALLY CAN MAKE YOU SEE SOMETHING THAT ISN'T THERE.

It's like magic!
But it's NOT magic! It's science! Wherever there are layers of air at different temperatures, light rays can bend, making a mirage.

It's not just seeing an oasis in the desert. Another type of mirage can make you see a ship floating in the sky!
WARMER AIR HIGHER UP
Yikes! A flying ship!
COLD AIR JUST ABOVE THE SEA
LIGHT RAYS COMING FROM A FARAWAY SHIP GET BENT...
AND IT LOOKS AS IF THE SHIP IS UP HERE!

I SAW A GHOSTLY SHIP....

It's true! I've seen it myself!

THERE ARE MANY OLD TALES OF SPOOKY FLYING GHOST SHIPS.

They were probably just mirages!

IS AN OASIS A REAL THING?

YES! DESERTS REALLY DO HAVE LITTLE LAKES FAR FROM RIVERS OR THE SEA, SURROUNDED BY PALM TREES, AND SOMETIMES A VILLAGE TOO.

IT RAINS OVER HERE
IN SOME PLACES, THE WATER FILLED-ROCKS SURROUND A DIP IN THE LAND, AND IT FILLS WITH WATER
WATER SOAKS INTO UNDERGROUND ROCKS AND SPREADS OUT BELOW THE SURFACE

GLOSSARY

AURORA GLOWING LIGHT THAT IS SOMETIMES IN THE NIGHT SKY AROUND THE POLES, CAUSED BY PARTICLES FROM THE SUN CRASHING INTO THE AIR.

COMPASS A DEVICE THAT SHOWS THE DIRECTION USING A MAGNETIC NEEDLE THAT LINES UP WITH EARTH'S POLES.

EQUATOR AN IMAGINARY DIVIDING LINE AROUND EARTH, HALFWAY BETWEEN THE TWO POLES.

GEYSER A KIND OF HOT SPRING THAT CAN BOIL OVER AND SHOOT OUT OF THE GROUND AS A BOILING HOT FOUNTAIN.

GRAVITY A FORCE THAT ALL OBJECTS HAVE, THAT PULLS OTHER OBJECTS TOWARD THEM.

HEADLAND A PIECE OF ROCKY LAND AT THE COAST THAT STICKS OUT INTO THE SEA.

LANDFORMS NATURAL SHAPES OR FEATURES OF EARTH'S SURFACE, LIKE CLIFFS, VALLEYS, AND MOUNTAINS.

MIGRATIONS LONG JOURNEYS THAT SOME ANIMALS MAKE TO FIND FOOD OR MEET A MATE.

MIRAGE A VISION OF SOMETHING THAT APPEARS IN THE WRONG PLACE, CAUSED BY LAYERS OF AIR BENDING LIGHT RAYS.

OASIS A POOL OF WATER IN A DESERT, MADE BY WATER STORED IN UNDERGROUND ROCKS.

PLATES THE HUGE SECTIONS OF ROCK THAT MAKE UP EARTH'S HARD SURFACE LAYER, OR CRUST.

PLUNGE POOL A DEEP POOL AT THE BOTTOM OF A WATERFALL, HOLLOWED OUT BY THE FORCE OF THE WATER.

POLES (NORTH POLE AND SOUTH POLE) THE MOST NORTHERN AND SOUTHERN POINTS ON EARTH. EARTH SPINS AROUND THE LINE BETWEEN THE TWO POLES.

SOLAR SYSTEM THE SUN AND ALL THE PLANETS, MOONS AND OTHER SPACE OBJECTS THAT ORBIT AROUND IT.

STATIC ELECTRICITY A FORM OF ELECTRICITY THAT CAN BUILD UP IN AN OBJECT OR MATERIAL, THEN JUMP OUT AS A SPARK OR A FLASH OF LIGHTNING.

TORNADO A VERY FAST, POWERFUL WINDSTORM THAT MOVES IN A NARROW SPIRAL.

QUIZ

1. EARTH IS A GIANT.... ?

A. CRYSTAL

B. MAGNET

C. POTATO

2. WHICH IS THE WORLD'S TALLEST MOUNTAIN, MEASURED FROM SEA LEVEL?

A. EVEREST

B. CHIMBORAZO

C. MAUNA KEA

3. WHICH OF THESE THINGS IS CAUSED BY THE MOON?

A. LIGHTNING

B. WATERFALLS

C. TIDES

4. HOW FAST DO THE GIANT PLATES THAT MAKE UP EARTH'S CRUST MOVE AROUND?

A. AS FAST AS A PASSENGER JET FLIES

B. AS FAST AS A SNAIL CAN SLITHER

C. AS FAST AS YOUR FINGERNAILS GROW

5. WHICH OF THESE HAS NOT FALLEN FROM THE SKY AS RAIN?

A. JELLYFISH

B. HORSES

C. TOADS

6. WHAT MAKES A GEYSER EXPLODE MORE EASILY?

A. SOAP

B. SOUP

C. SHEEP

7. WHAT'S THE NAME FOR A TOWER OF ROCK STANDING IN THE SEA?

A. A SKYSCRAPER

B. A STACK

C. A SPIRE

8. ONE OF THE EARLIEST COMPASSES EVER MADE WAS CALLED ... ?

A. THE SOUTH-POINTING FORK

B. THE SOUTH-POINTING CHEESE GRATER

C. THE SOUTH-POINTING SPOON

9. WHAT KIND OF PET WENT OVER NIAGARA FALLS IN A BARREL TO CHECK IT WAS SAFE?

A. A PET CAT

B. A PET DOG

C. A PET FISH

10. WHERE CAN A MIRAGE MAKE A SHIP APPEAR?

A. IN A PUDDLE

B. IN A TEACUP

C. IN THE SKY

ANSWERS: 1. B 2. A 3. C 4. C 5. B 6. A 7. B 8. C 9. A 10. C

INDEX

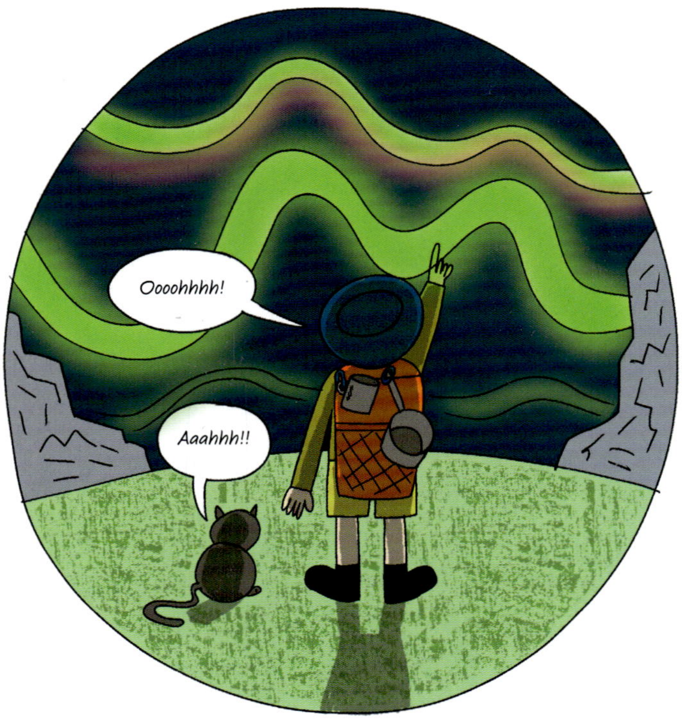
Oooohhhh!
Aaahhh!!